Social Communication Cues

for Young Children with

Autism Spectrum Disorders

and Related Conditions

of related interest

Motivate to Communicate!
300 Games and Activities for Your Child with Autism
Simone Griffin and Dianne Sandler
ISBN 978 1 84905 041 8

First Steps in Intervention with Your Child with Autism
Frameworks for Communication
Phil Christie, Elizabeth Newson, Wendy Prevezer and Susie Chandler
Illustrated by Pamela Venus
ISBN 978 1 84905 011 1

Learning About Friendship
Stories to Support Social Skills Training in Children with
Asperger Syndrome and High Functioning Autism
K.I. Al-Ghani
Illustrated by Haitham Al-Ghani
ISBN 978 1 84905 145 3

Liam Says "Hi"
Learning to Greet a Friend
Jane Whelen Banks
ISBN 978 1 84310 901 3

"As a clinician, I found *Social Communication Cues for Young Children with Autism Spectrum Disorders and Related Conditions* to be an incredibly useful hands-on guide for working as a social coach with children of all ages. As a parent of a child with social delays, I found it to be a blueprint for daily exercises and vocabulary that I could use at home and share with teachers. This book is a must-read for anyone who wants social skill-building tools at their fingertips."

—*Jennie Kaufman Singer, Ph.D., Licensed Clinical Psychologist and Assistant Professor, Sacramento State University, California*

both a parent and a professional I have found this approach be incredibly useful in breaking down the complexity of al exchanges. We often struggle for the right language convey the unwritten rules of engagement. This program s us the 'map' and consequently the confidence to help our dren. I'm encouraged by the progress I have witnessed!"

—*Nicole Mank, M.A., Marriage and Family Therapist and parent of a child with Sensory Processing Disorder, California*

"A in-depth look at social communication broken down i simplistic step-by-step instruction. While working with dren/young adults presenting with pragmatic language order, I have found that Varughese's program offers a rchical approach to pragmatic coaching and lends itself to seful for increasing the understanding and use of pragmatic lage at *any* age."

—*Michelle Harr, M.A., Speech-Language Pathologist, Michigan*

Social Communication Cues

for Young Children with

Autism Spectrum Disorders

and Related Conditions

How to Give Great Greetings, Pay Cool Compliments and Have Fun with Friends

Tarin Varughese

Jessica Kingsley *Publishers*
London and Philadelphia

First published in 2011
by Jessica Kingsley Publishers
116 Pentonville Road
London N1 9JB, UK
and
400 Market Street, Suite 400
Philadelphia, PA 19106, USA

www.jkp.com

Library of Congress Cataloging in Publication Data
Varughese, Tarin.
 Social communication cues for young children with autism spectrum disorders
and related conditions : how to give great greetings, pay cool compliments and
have fun with friends / Tarin Varughese.
 p. cm.
 Includes bibliographical references and index.
 ISBN 978-1-84905-870-4 (alk. paper)
 1. Autism in children--Treatment. 2. Language disorders in children--
Treatment. 3. Social skills in children. I. Title.
 RJ506.A9V37 2011
 618.92'85882--dc22
                                    2011001881

British Library Cataloguing in Publication Data
A CIP catalogue record for this book is available from the British Library

ISBN 978 1 84905 870 4

Printed and bound in Great Britain

Contents

Introduction

While social skills can best be learned in a social context, many children with Pervasive Developmental Disorder–Not Otherwise Specified (PDD–NOS), autism, Asperger's and/or Sensory Processing Disorder have been unable to learn social skills from environmental cues or experiences. Often these children require direct teaching and practice in order to obtain social competency. This program teaches a variety of skills that have been used and successfully gained by many children seen for speech-language services and social coaching. The program will help enhance the quality and scope of interactions that can be had with others, particularly peers.

As a pediatric speech-language pathologist, I have seen a multitude of children individually for therapy. While immensely beneficial in increasing children's receptive language (what they understand) and/or their expressive language (the language they use to make their wants and needs understood), over time it became clear that therapy was not enough. The children I saw were still relying on their parents or caregivers to communicate for them with other children. The bottom line is that children need to be able to communicate with their peers in order to be socially successful and independent.

It is a fact that children who have autism or Asperger's are particularly prone to developmental delays in the area of social skills. They are often unaware of social nuances, such as tone of voice, gestures, or body language. While more children are being seen for early intervention, including speech and language therapy services, these children are not necessarily being taught *how* to use the language they have learned socially, particularly with peers. This is potentially damaging to the self-esteem of any child.

The program in this book was created for children aged between three and seven years, and covers the following main categories needed for successful communication: Initiating Social Interaction, Maintaining Social Interaction, Body Positioning, Perspective Taking, Visual Modality, Emotional Regulations, and Development of Humor. Created for parents and professionals alike, this program is written in language that is accessible to anyone invested in the subject of social development.

Within this program, each of the chapters is arranged hierarchically from early developing skills to more challenging, later-developing social skills. Also, each of the topics covered offers readers vocabulary tips for verbally prompting children and how to then decrease these cues. Tips are also provided at the end of every section in order to help users increase generalization and carry over into other environments. Lastly, a social skills checklist is provided at the back of the book (see p.127) in order to help parents and professionals pinpoint areas of social skill need.

Who will benefit from socialization coaching tips?

- children with autism/spectrum disorders
- children with Sensory Processing Disorder
- children with social or generalized anxiety
- children with Pragmatic Language Disorder
- children who need help developing interaction skills (may act out or withdraw in social situations).

Please note that I have alternated between 'he' and 'she' in each chapter to describe an unspecified child. This is for the purposes of clarity only.

Chapter One

Initiating Social Interaction

Rule 1: Greeting Others

A child should be able to greet others (with gesture or verbally).

Reason

While difficult for many children, for those prone to anxiety this is a particularly difficult social skill. The ability to greet others independently is an important step toward social independence from parents, as children will no longer expect their parent's greeting to replace their own.

In social coaching sessions, we tell the children that what they do or say has an effect on the emotions of others. When a friend says "Hi" and they do not respond, they may make their friend feel awkward or sad, or assume that they are not interested in playing. When they respond appropriately by waving or saying "Hi," we explain that the other child's face will then often "light up."

Vocabulary

- Simply waving to a child without vocalizing then places mild social pressure on him to then respond, either with gesture or a verbal response, or both.

- Once the skill has been discussed and practiced, cue with "QUICK—Hi." The "QUICK" cue will be used intermittently throughout the program. Used with children who are prone to "freezing up" when confronted with an increase in sensory input, the "QUICK" cue is effective in helping redirect a child's attention and maintain social interaction.

TIPS

Take note of how the child responds to being greeted. Does he say "Hi" or wave to someone he knows? Do familiar people say "Hello" to the child, who then provides no response in return? Pay particular attention to the setting in which the child answers or does not. Does the child fail to respond more to peers than to adults?

Initially, a portable reward system is suggested, a token or something that can be taken around in one's pocket. When you see someone approaching, you can tell the child he has the chance to earn a reward by greeting the person. If he does, reward him with the token and then use this experience to build his self-confidence the next time he is greeted. ("Remember how you greeted Sam last week? Let's do it again.") If, however, he is not able to initiate a greeting, remind him there will be plenty of other opportunities for him to earn a reward.

Rule 2: Joint Attention

A child must get the attention of others before communicating (with body or verbally).

Reason

When a child with communication difficulties begins speaking before he truly has the attention of the person whom he is addressing, his message often goes unheard. When a child says something to another person, he needs to be sure he has the attention of his audience. This skill is self-reinforcing to children.

Vocabulary

Prompt with cues with the following:

- "Say his name."

- "Get his attention."

- Or "Tap his shoulder."

TIPS

Observe the child when he begins to speak to you or others around him. Is he aware whether the listener is facing him and making eye contact? Does he begin speaking without gaining joint attention? Joint attention is self-reinforcing for children because they begin to realize their wants are met much more consistently and more effortlessly if they have it. Frustration can be decreased dramatically for children with communication difficulties who learn joint attention. Suggested practice partners include parents, teachers, coaches, family members, and pets.

Rule 3: Asking for Help

A child needs to learn to initiate asking for help.

Reason

Children with social skill difficulties may have trouble speaking up and asking for help when they need it, whether from their parent, teacher or peer, but can learn how to do so with instruction. In social coaching sessions, we prompt the child by telling him what it is we are seeing, either on his face or using his body. For example, when we see a child who is trying to open something and cannot, we want to encourage him to then ask for help. Other children, such as those with significant anxiety, simply find themselves unable to utter the word "help". They often feel as though they should know how to do most things, despite the fact they are children.

Vocabulary

- Initially, we begin with having the young child motor imitate the sign for "help." "Motor imitation" refers to the ability of a child to imitate a gross or fine motor movement. (For example, imitating sign language requires a child to use their visual modality to motor imitate the hand movements observed.)

- For those emerging into the area of using the word "help" we might say, "You look frustrated. Did you want to ask a question?"

- With children who are beginning to generalize this skill, an adult might verbally cue the child with "I know how to do that. I've done it before," and then wait for the child to respond.

- As the concept is learned and emerging we cue with "Ask a question" if necessary.

TIPS

Observe whether or not the child feels comfortable verbally requesting help. Does he rely on push/pull or whining with parents rather than vocalizing his wants? Is he able to do so just with parents or with other adults as well? Is he able to ask another peer for help during play?

Try setting up situation in which a child would need to ask questions, such as by putting a toy up on a cupboard or tightening the lid on a jar. Then utilize the above vocabulary tips to elicit questions.

Rule 4: Responding to Comments

A child must respond to comments put out by his peers, either verbally or with gesture.

Examples

- "I saw a great movie this weekend…"

- "Hey, look at what I made."

Reason

Because some children do not pick up social cues on their own, they often need to be taught this particular rule. Teach the child that when someone shows you something or mentions something in passing about an experience, he is expected to respond to that particular item or topic. It is important to emphasize that his comment should be positive in nature and about the particular topic brought up, rather than changing the subject.

Vocabulary

- Instruct the child by plainly stating that he needs to "Stop, look, and Comment" about what his peer has just stated or give a gesture of acknowledgment.

- Or "You need to say something to your friend."

- Once the idea is understood, then cue with "Say something about your friend's [item/comment] or give him a thumbs up."

- After the skill emerges, decrease cue to "Think about your friend."

TIPS

Observe how your child responds when another child shows him something. Does he stop what he is doing to provide his peer with input? Does he change the subject to something unrelated to the object/comment?

To begin teaching this skill, an art project done in a group setting is a good way to structure the environment. Prompt children to share their creations with one another and observe their responses. Cue using the above vocabulary tips. Also, it is helpful to model this skill yourself for the child at home/in therapy.

Rule 5: Sharing Ideas/Accomplishments

A child needs to learn to share his creations and accomplishments with other children.

Reason

Children who experience social skill difficulties are not used to sharing their creations or successes with peers. They may be more inclined to show adults, however. We should really encourage our children to hold up their items of pride, and get the joint attention of peers, and then say something such as "Look, guys." This helps the children to grow in the area of human relatedness and is also self-esteem building.

Vocabulary

- Maximum prompt will be needed while teaching this rule, such as "Sometimes I say something like this, 'Look what I made.'"

- Once this skill emerges, prompt with "Show your friends."

- Also, later try gestures toward peers and say, "It's really nice. Show them."

TIPS

Observe your child over the next several days. Does he create something during play and then bring it to you and your attention for comment? If so, does he do so when playing with peers? This is important scaffolding for higher-level joint attention. (In this instance, "scaffolding" is the idea of presenting children with a "just right" social challenge and then increasing the level of difficulty slowly and incrementally as they are ready.)

It is also extremely self-reinforcing if children receive positive feedback from their peers. Again, an art or building project of some sort is a great way to set up a situation in which to teach and practice this rule.

Rule 6: Asking Questions

A child needs to learn to initiate asking questions rather than general statements in order to have his wants/needs met.

Reason

Young children seen for social coaching often communicate through the use of general statements, such as "I am hungry," rather than asking, "Can I have something to eat?" Or, even better, "Can I have a sandwich to eat?" At age four and above the ability to ask questions is socially appropriate and empowering for children. Using questions will help them to get their needs met better. Asking questions allows them to create conversation and learn more about the world around them. When children gain joint attention from another individual, and then request what they want specifically, their efforts will be reinforced, and generalization of this skill to other environments will occur.

Vocabulary

- While teaching this rule, begin with "You need to ask a question. Can I have…"

- "Are you asking me a question?"

- "Ask me a WHERE question." Or "Ask me a WHAT question."

- Cue by starting the question for them: "Can I…"

- Fading cues would consist of the visual only sign for letter "C" to prompt for "Can." (Fading cues refers to decreasing the verbal, visual, or tactile cues the adult provides to aid the child in hitting a particular goal.)

TIPS

As children develop, they need to be aware of the type of utterances they produce. The skill of asking questions shows greater cognitive complexity in their development than commenting. This week, listen closely to how the child expresses himself. Is he making his wants and needs understood clearly by asking a question of another party? Is he using one-word utterances to get items, such as "Milk?" Or does he employ push/pull or whining to request items? If he is not asking questions consistently, cue them with the above vocabulary.

Rule 7: Getting Clarification

A child needs to learn to initiate asking questions for purposes of clarification.

Reason

Children with social skill delays often have difficulty initiating questions to clarify a misunderstanding. For example, a young girl recently related to her social coach that she was very sad about something that had happened earlier in the day at school. She was lining up to leave and was behind two boys. The boys used language she did not like and she somehow assumed they were talking about her. However, after later reflecting back, the child realized the two boys' bodies were turned away from her while lining up and agreed that they were probably not talking to or about her.

In session, we worked with that particular child on simply asking, "Were you talking about me?" The need to check in and clarify is huge for children with social skill challenges. This then frees them up emotionally and allows them to then be more "present." Feeling comfortable asking questions is an important tool for children; it can help him gain a sense of control as well as safety when away from their home environment.

Vocabulary

- "Can you say that again?" or "What did you mean?"

- When a child has difficulty knowing if someone is just laughing or if he is being laughed at, the prompt "Do a double check" is very useful. The child is then to follow up by asking, "Were you laughing at me?"

TIPS

Observe how the child reacts when unsure of what is being said, reading facial expressions or the body posture of others. Help him to feel more comfortable about asking for clarification by talking with him about the importance of this skill. Perhaps modeling you and other family members doing so when at home or out in the community will show them that this is helpful and does not have to be scary.

Rule 8: Asking Someone to Play

A child needs to learn how to ask peers to play with them.

Reason

For children who remain in parallel play (playing independently alongside, rather than with, another child) or are used to playing on their own at home and during recess time, it is often difficult to take the "next step" to ask another child to play with them. It often helps to have a specific game in mind when approaching another child. For example, a social coach might encourage the child to say, "Do you want to play trains with me?" or "Do you want to play handball with me?" Older children, such as first graders, may hesitate out of fear of being rejected. Social coaching will help them identify other people who have the same interests, and how to practice approaching these individuals.

Vocabulary

- When teaching this skill cue with "Ask them, 'Do you want to play [game].'"

- "Ask your friends if they want to play [game] with you."

- "Ask your friend a question."

TIPS

Does the child prefer to play on his own? Does he prefer to have control over the items he is playing with? Does he get nervous or agitated if another child approaches him during play? Or, perhaps, does he want to interact with another peer, but seem unsure of how to ask another child to join him? Help prompt him with the vocabulary provided above, particularly if the other child seems like she would reciprocate.

Rule 9: Initiating Conversation

A child needs to be able to initiate conversation with peers.

Reason

As early as preschool, it is healthy for children to share themselves and their ideas with peers. For children who struggle with anxiety, drawing attention to themselves is something they avoid, despite the fact that they do have things they would like to share with others. Often, our children do much better initiating social conversation with adults than peers. During social coaching we attempt to pull out from them the commonalities between peer group members, be it age, school situations, sibling challenges, music interests, toy preferences, etc. Finding similarities can help open up a child and give him topics to discuss with peers.

Vocabulary

- Initially you will see a child share something (event or object) with you or another adult, but not peers. Prompt them by saying, "That is very interesting. You should tell the group."

- Finally, "QUICK—Tell your friends!"

TIPS

When present with children in a group setting, you may often overhear portions of conversation. When a subject comes up that you know your child is excited about/comfortable with/knowledgeable about, you might then help prompt him by using the above vocabulary. The positive response of the other children can be the child's positive reinforcement. Also, revisiting the situation afterwards can also help the child by decreasing his anxiety about sharing ideas with peers. You might say, "I was proud of how you told your friend(s) about the [event/item]. They seemed to really be interested in that also."

Rule 10: Repairing Misunderstandings

A child needs to develop the skill of social repair when a misunderstanding occurs.

Reason

Children with social skill delays are often unsure of how to repair a social misunderstanding, both with adults and peers. While adults can be an easier "audience," peers are often tougher for our children. Regardless of whether self-esteem or the desire to not make the other person feel poorly is the root cause, we want our kids to be verbally confident. We want them to know truly within themselves that they do have control over their own internal and external environment at the moment when the incident occurs.

Vocabulary

After discussing this particular rule with a child, you can then cue them by verbally prompting with the following:

- "Ask them, 'What do *you* mean?'."

- Or "Tell them, 'That's not what *I* meant'."

TIPS

Observe the child's interactions with peers. Is he more prone than his typically developing peers to freeze, fight, flight or combinations thereof? It is paramount that the child understands that he actually has control over social situations, not by use of his body, but by formulation of his words and ideas. Discuss the topic of misunderstandings with the child. Guide him by using the above vocabulary when you are present for such social situations. Later, revisit the situation and discuss when not in the heat of the moment. (This is also a good time to discuss embarrassment, e.g. that while it is a difficult emotion, it occurs and then diminishes thereafter. It does not last forever.)

Chapter Two

Maintaining Social Interaction

Rule 1: Small Transitions

A child must be able to make small transitions in order for play/interactions to be most successful.

Reason

The ability to transition can be broken down into a multitude of steps. Take, for example, a child with sensory processing difficulties who may have trouble transitioning away from a toy she is investigating with hyperdiligence. These are often the children who are still playing even after the teacher has given several warnings to clean up. They are preoccupied with their sensory world, and therefore when they are approached and the toy is removed from their hands they become very upset. They missed the previous cues to transition. This is something that with scaffolding can be helped tremendously through social coaching. With development of a common vocabulary used at home, in class, and out in the community, the children we see become better able to utilize taught strategies.

Vocabulary

- In the beginning a child may require physical prompt, such as a firm input/pressure to her shoulder to get her attention, then verbal cues of "Stop. Look. Listen."

- Then decrease cues to "Stop. Look. Listen" without tactile cues.

- Then paired down further to "Stop. Look."

- Finally, fade cue to simply "Stop."

TIPS

Thinking of transitions as something that can be scaffolded into a myriad of steps can often be helpful for parents and professionals. Often we think of transitions of larger movements of our body from one environment to another. For some of the population of children we see, moving from one toy or task to another can cause freeze, fight, or flight.

Rule 2: Large Transitions

A child must be able to make large transitions in order for play/interactions to be most successful.

Reason

For children with anxiety, for example, transitions represent the unknown and the unexpected. These are the children who prefer to stay at home, and look forward to weekends at home. For them, the predictable nature of the home environment is most desirable. Unfortunately, life is full of continuous transitions. Use of strategies can help decrease these children's anxiety through an increased feeling of control over their environment.

Vocabulary

- *Carrier objects:* "What can you take with you in the car that you can take into the classroom to share?" This helps build for a child a mental picture of what she might be doing with her school day. This is also very helpful when going to a social event. If a child brings two toys in her pocket, she will then have something to do and can offer another to another child. This then immediately creates a parallel play situation, which is more likely to develop into more cooperative play with time.

- *Schedule boards:* Given a visual representation of how their day is going to look can be very calming for many children, and can help with larger transitions. Schedule boards also take out some of the unexpected factors in a child's day, thereby decreasing her overall level of anxiety.

- *Verbal rehearsal:* Parents and professionals are urged to use visual imagery with children who have difficulties with anxiety. A mental picture of a situation helps prepare the child for what is to come. A Plan A, B, and C can also be included in the rehearsal in order to help with flexibility.

TIPS

Make a list of transitions that are most difficult for the child. Begin to think of visual cues that might help ease these tough situations. Use of a schedule and verbal rehearsal can help offset the unexpected nature of transitions and help diffuse anxiety for a child with special needs.

Rule 3: Maintaining Play

A child must learn to maintain play once initiating interaction with peers.

SCENARIO ONE

Reason

Because some children have not had experience with true reciprocal play they are unsure how to maintain a game or interaction once it has begun. While they may be able to ask a child to play, they may then "freeze." An example of this is when we see a child allowing her peer to take out a game and set it up alone, rather than helping do so. In session, we provide a safe environment for the children to practice asserting themselves during play. If only one child proceeds to take out the game to set up, we may ask her to put it back. This can be explained by stating, "Can you put it back and let your friend practice?"

Vocabulary

Cue the reserved/anxious child with "Pick one thing to set up."

TIPS

In this particular scenario, we support children by providing ideas for them, such as giving them one task to perform to help set up the game, so that they are not overwhelmed by the overall process.

SCENARIO TWO

Reason

Another example we see quite often is when a child asks another to play, and then proceeds to dominate the interaction. This child can be observed choosing the game, setting it up herself, and then going first without "checking in" with her friend.

Vocabulary

- Using a confused face, prompt with "Wait. Look at your friend's face. They look confused."

- "How can we change this so that you are playing together?"

- Or, with older children we may say, "Wait. Check in with your friend."

TIPS

Watch how the child asks another peer to play and then follow how the interaction unfolds. Does your child feel the need to dominate or control the flow of play to the point that the other child begins to feel uncertain? Prompt with the above vocabulary.

Rule 4: Turn-Taking

A child must be able to take turns during play.

Reason

The ability to take turns during a game is crucial to the development of successful maintenance of play. When a child is either unable to share turns or unwilling to take her turn, but would rather watch, play is one-sided and often momentum is lost. This particular rule is best taught when playing with just one other child so that the wait time between turns is minimal for the child. Once mastered, adding another peer in the play increases the level of difficulty.

Note: Turn-taking is also developmentally important for our youngest clients, who may also have a speech and language delay. Verbal turn-taking can be taught or emulated through use of turn-taking during play.

Vocabulary

- After discussing turn-taking and its importance, a social coach might say to a child, "It makes your friend happy when you let her take her own turn."

- Or "Tell your friend, 'Your turn!'" or "Tell your friend, 'It's my turn!'" in order to continue the flow of the play when sharing is a challenge.

TIPS

While some parents shy away from turn-taking game play, as it can often result in a meltdown for many young children, it is crucial to every child's social and emotional development. Simple games and board games (such as Snakes and Ladders) can help your child learn to take turns, knowing that it will only be a set increment of time until it is her turn once again. When playing a board game with a child with special needs, parents are encouraged to play fair and not let the child win on purpose as this act, if done consistently, can create a false expectation for the child that she will always win. It is important to create a situation that may realistically occur so that the child has more practice handling the emotions of winning and losing in a safe environment.

Rule 5: Watching Peers at Play

A child needs to watch their peers take their turn while playing games.

Reason

Often perspective-taking stands in the way of many children following the flow of peer interaction when turn-taking is involved. (Please refer also to Chapter 4 for further information.) While children with social skill deficits may want children to watch them take their turn, once their *own* turn is over they stop attending to the game at hand. Social coaching can help children understand the importance of this rule. Attending to the game allows for the child to know when her turn is coming back around. It also prompts her to be in tune with how her peers are feeling during the flow of the game. Lastly, it helps maintain the flow of play.

Vocabulary

- A direct cue would be "Fix your body. Watch your friend take their turn."

- An indirect cue would be "It makes your friend feel so good when you watch her take her turn."

- Decrease cue to "Use your eyes."

TIPS

Become more aware of how the child interacts when involved in an organized game with peers, such as a board game or other turn-taking games. After her own turn, does she begin to wiggle and turn away from the board game? Help her to focus and attend by using the above vocabulary tips.

The use of fidget toys may be helpful for some children who need sensory input or who are anxious waiting for their turn. Fidget toys are made of a variety of materials, often stretchy in nature, and can be used to keep a child's hands busy and provide sensory input so that she can attend better in a group situation.

Rule 6: Organizing Play

A child needs to know how to get a game/play organized.

Reason

Negotiation is often needed at the onset of play. When in a group it is important that older children communicate with one another while choosing a game and establishing the rules. Discussions may also come up during the game, when one child might want to change a rule previously set. In a recent first-grade boys' group, a social coach helped set up the rules for a game of "Sorry." While three boys were present, one boy in particular attempted to change the rules of the game each and every time it was his turn. This was a very telling event and an important window of learning for him and his group.

Vocabulary

At this level of complexity with social coaching, social coaches act more as a safety net, nudging the children along, helping them to use their plan B, C, and D. Vocabulary used might be variations of the following:

- "Talk to your friends. Decide as a group."

- "Does everyone know the rules? What are they?"

TIPS

When interacting with friends or family, does the child often change the rules of the game after play has already started? Does she attempt to change the rules during each turn? This is a time in which you might instruct her to "Check in with your friends" and see if all of these new rules are okay with the group as a whole. It is often helpful to set the rules before beginning so that each child is clear on them. The group can also decide together if the rules can be changed during the game, to avoid confusion later.

Rule 7: Deciding Who Goes First

A child needs to have strategies for deciding who goes first.

Reason

Children who have social learning delays often have difficulty when it comes to starting a game, and, more specifically, deciding who goes first. Practicing different ways of deciding helps give the children ideas so that play is maintained. Examples of ways to decide who goes first include picking a number between 1 and 10, doing Rock-Paper-Scissors, going youngest to oldest, or flipping a coin.

Vocabulary

"How can we decide who goes first?"

TIP ONE

Often as parents, when playing a game, we let children go first. However, this may not be the best solution for helping our children who have social difficulties. Perhaps assert yourself during a task by saying, "But I want to go first, too. What can we do?" This will let them practice for when it occurs with peers and they are unsure of how to respond.

Vocabulary

"QUICK—Go!"

TIP TWO

On the flip side, we do also see children who will not go first. They will actually insist on going last. It may be because they are afraid they won't know how to play and are hesitant to ask how, or it might be that their anxiety increases with the idea of having to go first, or it may just be the desire for control. With these particular children a social coach might ease the way with "Here are the rules. Okay, you start [name]." Again this is the idea of the power "QUICK," followed by reassurance of "You can do it."

Rule 8: Negotiating

A child needs to pursue her wants/needs through negotiation and verbal persistence.

Reason

Children with social skill delays often have trouble with verbal turn-taking. Here is an example we see regularly. A child may ask another child for a turn with a toy or game. If told "No, I am using it," we may see a child walk away and not pursue it any longer or she may become very angry. We often prompt her to "Ask the next question", meaning she should not give up, but keep working toward what it is she wants. For example, she could then say, "Can I have it after you?" or "Can I have it when you are done?"

Vocabulary

- If a child attempts to grab things out of someone else's hands, social coaching for this task might begin with simply explaining to the child, "Oh! Just so you know, you can't do that."

- Further cuing would be for the child to "Ask if you can have a turn." If told no, prompt her with "Ask the next question. Can I have it after you?"

- Decrease cue to "Ask the next question."

- Also, the use of the "waiting hand" (palm up) is stressed. A patient waiting hand can be influential, whereas reaching out to grab a toy is offputting for other children.

TIPS

What do you observe at home, school, or while out on play dates when a child wants something someone else is holding. Is she able to initiate a question? If told no, what does she do? Is she tempted to pull a toy out of another child's hand? This is a window for learning in that a parent can try to pair the face the other child is making with the actions of the child's hands pulling the toy away.

Rule 9: Navigating a "Bump in the Road"

A child needs to learn how to maintain play once a "bump in the road" occurs.

Reason

In order to maintain play, a child must know how to get past misunderstandings or "bumps in the road" during play. For example, some children have difficulty knowing where their body is in space, secondary to sensory processing difficulties. These children lack proper registration when they bump, sit on, trip over, or knock down another child's toy. During these instances they exhibit difficulty stopping and acknowledging their mistake and making amends with peers. Other children who have social anxiety believe that if they do not mention the incident, then perhaps no one noticed and no hurt feelings were had. With these children social coaching fosters the idea of acknowledgment and then quickly moving on with the game. Other children simply *do not know* to stop and quickly repair the moment, but they can quickly be taught to do so.

Vocabulary

- A child with decreased body awareness may need to be cued verbally to be made aware of her position in space. Cue with "Uh oh. Look down! What can you say to your friend?"

- A child with high anxiety may need help acknowledging and then moving on quickly. Try cuing with "Freeze. Let's do that again! QUICK—Sorry./QUICK—Excuse me." Later decrease cue to "QUICK—Sorry."

- After teaching a child who is not aware of the need to acknowledge an incident or how to do so, cue with "What can you say to your friend?"

TIPS

Observe the child in a variety of social situations. When an awkward moment or an accident occurs, is she able to stop, acknowledge and move on? Or does she ignore the incident and move away from the place in which it occurred? As you begin to pinpoint trouble times, such as with peer interactions v. interactions with adults, help cue the child with whichever elements of the above vocabulary you feel most comfortable.

Rule 10: Exiting a Game

A child must learn how to exit or end a game when with a group.

Reason

When a child no longer wants to partake in a game, social rules dictate that she does not simply get up and walk away. She needs to be able obtain joint attention with the peers she is playing with and tell them she doesn't want to play any longer. When she is part of a group, she needs to check in with friends to see if they look like they are done with a game, too, based on facial expressions and body positioning. Maintaining play includes the transition from one game to the next during play.

Vocabulary

- Social coaches may cue by saying, "I don't want to play any more. Do you?"

- Then follow up with "Do you want to play a different game with me?" so that play can be maintained.

TIPS

Observe how your child exits a game or play interaction. Does she let others know she is done playing? Does she check in to see whether her friends are done, too? Use the suggested vocabulary tips to help guide her in doing so. This will help with maintaining play, by choosing another game to play with the same friends.

Chapter Three

Body Positioning

Rule 1: Staying with the Group

A child must understand the idea of being part of a group and the importance of staying with their group.

Reason

Children with pragmatic or social skills difficulties are focused on what they themselves are doing, saying, or thinking. As a result, they may simply get up and leave a group to go to the bathroom or get a toy in another room. It is important for all children to realize that when they are in a group, they have a responsibility to others present. When in a group, they should take into consideration the feelings of others (see Chapter Four). Teaching children the difference between playing on their own versus playing with peers helps distinguish what is expected of them socially.

Vocabulary

- "Keep your body in the group!"

- As this skill emerges, decrease cue later to "Fix your body."

- A visual cue of confusion, perhaps dramatized by the social coach, can then be used to help the child focus in on what is expected of him.

TIPS

Talk with your child about the idea of playing on his own, versus when he is in a group, such as with peers. Verbally discuss how these two situations are different. How do they look different? How would their body positioning differ if he was alone versus if he was in a social situation with peers? Pretend play with figures can help the child see the difference between the situations, while removing the emotions outside of themselves.

Rule 2: Exiting the Group

A child must let the whole group know that they are leaving before doing so.

Reason

When one is in a group setting, one needs to let others know before leaving the group (to go to a rest room, to fetch a tissue, etc.) When in a group, children must learn that they have a responsibility to the others, and are important to the group. Social coaching is used to instruct the children to let a peer group know if they need to go and do something, or if they are done playing a game before exiting. To help make this point clear, a social coach will act out this rule by abruptly getting up and leaving the group, and then the other social coach will draw attention to this odd behavior. Often, the children themselves are quick to protest when an adult acts inappropriately, but not as readily with peers.

Vocabulary

- Cue with "Tell them, 'Hey guys, I will be right back.'"

- Decrease cue to "Wait, I am confused… Can you explain?"

- If done playing a game, cue with "Tell your friend, 'I am done playing this now.'"

TIPS

Taught early, this rule can help children know what is expected when in a group and feel more comfortable navigating their way socially. Some children simply need to have this rule explained to them. As with Body Positioning Rule 1, play acting is a good way to practice this particular skill in a positive, fun, and non-threatening way.

Even within the home environment, we urge families to help build the construct for their children that the family *is* indeed a group. Before exiting the dinner table, play room, movie-watching night, etc. they are responsible for letting their family know they are done.

Rule 3: Body Positioning

A child needs to be aware of the positioning of his body in relation to others.

Reason

When in a group setting, children must be aware of how they position their body in relation to other children in order to successfully interact and engage in play. Sometimes children will get absorbed in a toy and inadvertently find themselves with their back to the main group. Some children will position their body away from a group in the attempt to lessen the amount of sensory input that they have to endure. Here is an example for adults of how slight the nuances are of body positioning. When two people are talking to one another, society dictates that we walk around them rather than walking between them. With older children social coaches sometimes explain to them, "We do not want your friend to think that you are meaning to be rude...because we know you are not a rude person."

Vocabulary

- After discussing this rule with the child, cue with "Fix your body."

- Once the skill emerges, decrease the cue to "Look at your body."

TIPS

Discuss this rule with the child. Explain that you do not want others to think he is being rude, because he is not a rude child. When he is then in a group situation and you observe the child turned with his body away from the group, or perhaps walking into the center, you can help repair this by gently cuing him with the above vocabulary. Also, play acting is a good way to help children learn the skills they need to succeed. For example, a parent who is turned away from a child, but still talking to him, is extremely noticeable even to a child with social skill challenges.

Rule 4: Using Your Words Not Your Body

Children must use their words, not their body, when interacting with others.

Reason

In order to be socially happy it is very important that all children learn to verbally express themselves, rather than relying on physicality. In younger children, such as preschoolers, we might see a child push a peer off of a piece of equipment because he wanted to use it, rather than asking for a turn. Another example of this is the child playing a card game who does not tell peers "It's your turn" or "Take your turn, please..." but reaches over and takes their turn for them, by pulling a card out of the other child's hand and placing it on the stack. While developmentally appropriate at a young age, if not extinguished this use of one's body rather than words can keep peers from wanting to play with these children.

Vocabulary

- After explaining this rule, cue with "Freeze. Ask your friend a question."

- Then decrease cue to "Freeze. Ask him in a different way."

- Finally, "Try again."

TIPS

Is the child able to use his words rather than his body to communicate his wants? Does the use of his body occur more with family members than in outside environments such as the classroom? The answers to these questions can be determined based on parent interview, teacher interview, client interview and observation. This will help in targeting the skill more directly.

Rule 5: Asking and Waiting for the Answer

When a child does ask a peer for a toy/object, he must wait for a response.

Reason

A child with social skill delays can be preoccupied with his own wants and needs, so much so that they may ask a question but not wait to hear the answer. An example of this is when a child asks to use a toy, does not wait for the answer, and grabs it. Having something taken out of one's hands is disturbing to most people, children and adults alike. Learning to ask a question and then practicing putting a hand out, palm up, gives your child a routine to follow and replaces his previous habit of grabbing. The sight of an open palm often encourages another child to share with peers.

Vocabulary

- After explaining this rule, cue with "Look for the answer."

- Also, if the child is waiting for an object, cue with "Put your hand out, palm up, and wait."

- Then decrease this cue to "Waiting hand."

TIPS

After explaining this rule, a silly game can be made out of "looking for the answer." For example, the adult can make funny faces that will entice the young child to watch their face. This in turn will help the child to attach a positive feeling to making eye contact and help him to learn to read facial expressions. When successful, this task is a self-reinforcing one.

Note: Refer to Chapter Two when a peer does not agree to share a toy or game.

Rule 6: Personal Space

Children need to be aware of the space between their body and others.

Reason

Many of us have a certain level of personal space which we need in order to feel comfortable. Some children, perhaps those who desire sensory input and/or lack body awareness, find themselves within too close a proximity to other people's personal space. By teaching the idea of how much room each person needs by visually showing them with our arms out in front we can help children become more successful socially.

We may also exaggerate our facial expressions and the retreat of our upper body when they come at us quickly so that they may be more aware of their intrusion.

Vocabulary

- After explaining this rule, cue with "Whoa! Too close. Fix your body."

- Later decrease cue to "Fix your body."

- If the child happens to be reaching over a peer or social coach to obtain something, cue with "Ask a question."

TIPS

Personal space is a concept that is appropriate for all preschoolers to begin understanding. One way in which to make a game out of teaching this skill is to have each child use a hula hoop to dictate the amount of space they are most comfortable with and then play a game in which they are standing and moving, such as Cranium® Hullabaloo.

Note: As a parent we want the affection of our kids. It is important to distinguish between closeness and perhaps interactions that others might find to be intrusive. As parents, we want to help our children practice in order to be successful when they are away from us.

Chapter Four

Perspective-Taking

Rule 1: Thinking About Others

Children need to develop the ability to think about the likes/dislikes of others.

Reason

Often children can be absorbed inwards by how they and their bodies are feeling. This then does not allow them the luxury of thinking about others. Rule 1 is a very important first step to achieving social perspective. Begin by simply asking the child to think about others when those people are not present. For example, have her think about something that might make a peer feel good, such as a toy, or something that might make her feel scared, such as bugs.

In social coaching sessions we may scaffold by having her think about her group peer member while that person is present. Later, we have the child think about others who are not present. For example, if a peer is absent from the group that day we might say, "Let's think about [peer's name]. How do you think he is feeling about having to miss the group today? What are two things he could be doing now?"

Vocabulary

- After discussing this skill, cue the children by saying, "Look at [peer], what do we know about her?"

- Later when the person is not present, cue the child to "Think about [peer]. What do you think she might like/dislike about [situation]?"

TIPS

When out at the store, pretend to play a game with your child. Ask her, "What would [name] like from that store? What do we know about him?" Get her thinking about others in this manner. While it does not always mean you have to be buying something for someone, it is interesting to further this assignment by bringing something back to the person whom the child was asked to think about. The child then sees first-hand how the object (i.e. book, picked flowers, coffee) actually did really make that person

---

feel good, simply because the child was thinking about her. Pairing the person's facial expressions with the fact that the child made the person feel and react in such a way is very powerful and self-reinforcing.

Rule 2: Use of Pronouns

A child must develop use of pronouns that reflect perspective-taking.

Reason

Children who display social skill delays often continue to use the pronouns "I" and "me" long past what is developmentally appropriate. For example, during play you might hear a child say, "I don't like this game." In session we try to turn these types of comments toward the group by encouraging them to say instead or additionally, "Are *you* guys all done?" or "Do you guys want to play this same game any longer?" This provides these children with the opportunity to then stop and read their friends' expressions and gain perspective about how their friends feel about a certain game. Also, when in a group, they need to think of themselves as part of the whole. Observing a child's use of pronouns ("I" and "me" versus "we" and "us") is extremely telling regarding a child's perspective-taking abilities.

Vocabulary

- After the specific concept is taught, begin coaching with "Try... Do you..." or "Can we..."

- Later, decrease cue to "Can you ask your friend/ him a question?"

TIPS

Observe the child over the next couple of days. Observe what pronouns she uses most often. Do statements begin with "I want..." most of the time? When a child uses "you," "we," or "us" it shows there is a perspective shift that is very important for her overall development.

When interacting with the child, guide her into using perspective-taking pronouns such as "you," "we," and "us." Use the above vocabulary tips to help prompt the shift in pronoun use and decrease as soon as emergence of this skill begins.

Rule 3: Positioning of Objects/Items

Children should be aware of the positioning of objects in relation to themselves and others when in a group.

Reason

When interacting with peers, it is important that all children have access to the board game or toy that is being shared. Unfortunately, at this level of perspective-taking we see children holding their own wants and needs as the primary focus, even when in a group of peers. For example, we may see a child remove a game from its box and then place it next to herself rather than in the middle of the group where everyone can reach it. She will then proceed to open the box and remove game items until instructed to "Freeze" by social coaches.

Vocabulary

- After social skill is discussed cue with, "Freeze. Use your eyes and look around. Can [name] reach it, too?"

- Decrease cue to "Freeze. Look around at your friends. Fix it."

- Finally, cue with "Freeze," and then gesture for the child to observe the group.

TIPS

Observe the child and see how she positions an object which she has said she wants to share with you. For example: Is the game to the right of her body, rather than in between you and the child? Does she show you a picture she made but hold it up for viewing with the picture facing her, not you? This rule is a skill that many children with social skill delays need to be taught directly.

Rule 4: Affecting Emotions of Others

Children need to understand that their words and gestures can affect the emotions of others.

Reason

When perspective-taking and/or impulse control is challenging for a child, she often needs help developing her internal filter. By systematically teaching children that the words they use with family and friends have an impact on others, they can control whether they have friends. In social coaching we teach children the art of filtering by learning to make neutral comments. For example, if a child is taught that if someone got a very bad haircut perhaps that person may think so too and be feeling bad, this will help give them others' perspectives. The child would then be cued to adjust her comment from "Bad haircut!" to "Don't worry. Your hair grows back fast."

Vocabulary

- After discussing this rule, cue the child to "Think about the other person's feelings."

- Decrease cue then to "Stop and think about your friend."

- We can tell a child who is prone to thoughts that might hurt another's feelings that she can "Keep that thought in your head," but not say it out loud.

TIPS

When children with social skill needs say something that is awkward and not well received by others, we really need to help them understand where the disconnect occurred. If we can do so in the moment that is great for understanding ("How did her face look after you said that?"). Often, however, the exact moment of an embarrassing situation is not the time nor a safe place emotionally for children to discuss their social errors. It is suggested that once the child is calm and able to talk about it she does so. This is considered an opportunity for social learning.

Rule 5: Acknowledging Comments

When a peer holds up an object for others to see, a child must make a comment about that particular object.

Reason

When another child holds something up or makes a comment upon something that she wants to share, society dictates that those around her respond in some manner about the topic introduced. While learning this skill falls also in the realm of maintaining play and interactions, the root of the deficit involved is lack of perspective-taking. Often it is due to the fact that children with social skill delays simply do not know they were expected to stop and comment. Those who have difficulty with this rule may still be learning that the words they use have a direct effect on others, either good or bad.

Vocabulary

- After discussing this skill, cue with "What can we say about your friend's [object]?"

- If more cuing is needed, help prompt with ideas, such as thumbs up, smiling and nodding, "Good job", "Nice work", or even "Wow!"

- As time goes by, decrease cues to simply "Stop. Look. What can you say to your friend?"

- Again decrease prompt to "What can you say?"

TIPS

It is important to point out to the child that her response made her friend feel good. Pairing a child's verbalization with the friend's positive affect is greatly helpful. This helps the child learn that what she says has an effect on those around her. Plan an art project with a child and a peer or two. Have them each go around and share their work with the group.

Rule 6: Reading Body Cues

A child needs to use her eyes to verbally identify how another person may be feeling based on social nuances.

Reason

In order successfully to take the perspective of another, a child must use her visual modality to observe the facial expressions, gestures, and body postures of others. The clues gained by observing these nuances will allow your child to move forward in her overall social development.

When taught, this particular rule should be broken down further. For example, many children with social delays do not truly know what their own face looks like when they express emotions. As a result, they are then unsure of what facial expressions mean on others. Therefore, this rule should be systematically taught to children with special needs.

Vocabulary

- When discussing their emotions, cue with "Your face/body is telling me you feel [emotion]. Is that right?"

- When discussing the emotions of peers, cue with "Your friend seems [label emotion]. What could we say to them?"

- Or "Look at her face. What is it telling us?"

TIPS

When at an event or out on errands, observe the child and how she reacts/does not react when a situation of high emotion occurs in front of her. How is she affected? Does she seem to notice? If she does not, as parents and educators we can draw the child's attention to the event (at the time of or after the fact) by narrating out loud through our own perspective. For example, if you spot someone who is frustrated while in line, you could quietly tell the child, "Wow. Did you see that woman's face? She looked frustrated with the long line..." This lends your child her own internal dialogue. Discussing aloud with her your own internal dialogue is a good way of helping children better understand facial expressions and body posture.

Rule 7: Clarifying "Why Are You Laughing?"

Children need to be able to clarify whether there just happens to be laughter occurring around them or if they are indeed being laughed at by another.

Reason

Children with social skill deficits, particularly those secondary to Sensory Processing Disorder or autism spectrum disorder, can often misread laughter as they are not always in tune with auditory and visual cues. When a joke is made while they are present they may miss it, and they feel they have missed something. As a result, these children then go straight to assuming they are being laughed at by peers. During social coaching sessions we explain the need to simply stop and address a peer in such a situation.

Vocabulary

- After having discussed this rule cue with "Ask them, 'Are you laughing at me?'"

- Or "What is funny?"

- "What did I miss?"

- Once the concept is emerging, decrease cue to "Do a double check."

TIPS

As parents and educators, we have all seen mis-understandings such as this occur. When children think that others are laughing at them, when in fact they were not really even part of that particular dia-logue, they may either go straight to freeze, flight, or fight. This stage is typical for most three- and four-year-olds, but the children who remain in this stage suffer greatly in social situations. As they get older, their behavior becomes more curious or fearful of their peers. We feel that these children then need extra help to support them in these tough situations.

Use the above vocabulary tips to begin working on this rule. Doing so will give children a "back-up plan" for when such a situation occurs. It will also give them a sense of control within their social environment.

Rule 8: Expressing Empathy

A child needs to show empathy with others.

Reason

Social rules dictate that we show concern for others and doing so is a social necessity for successful interactions. Having the skills to be able to understand, be aware of, or be sensitive to what another person is feeling is a stepping stone to good perspective-taking. Demonstrating that you can "put yourself in another person's shoes" without experiencing what is causing the thoughts or feelings the other person is facing, and then reacting in a comforting manner, can be considered a higher level of social connectedness. Through social coaching children learn that when in a group, they have a responsibility to "check in" with their friends regarding how they are feeling. Practicing this skill in a safe, supported environment, such as a social skill group, gives the child tools to interact comfortably.

Vocabulary

- After teaching this lesson, cue the child by drawing her attention to the situation in front of her, such as "Your friend just [action]. What can we say to him?"

- Decrease cue thereafter to "What can we say to your friend?"

TIPS

Pretend play is a good way to practice empathetic responses. Many children with social skill difficulties need to practice out loud responses that are expected from others, in order to become comfortable doing so with adults and peers. For example, when another person trips and falls or bumps into something, we ask if she is okay. Or if a person is coughing profusely, we ask if she needs water.

Chapter Five

Visual Modality

Rule 1: Listening with Eye Contact

Children need to use eye contact when listening to others.

Reason

Decreased eye contact negatively effects communication. Children who have decreased eye contact miss a great deal of social information. Later on in the development of a child, lack of eye contact will cause him to miss a great deal of academic information provided in the classroom by the teacher or on the blackboard. For a fully integrated system to work effectively, children must use both their eyes and their ears when interacting with the world and people around them.

Vocabulary

- For younger children cue with "It makes me happy when you look at my face," or "It makes your friends feel good when you look at them."

- For older children cue with "I feel like you care about what I am saying when you look at me."

- Once skill is emerging, decrease cues to "Use your eyes."

TIPS

Does the child make eye contact with you, friends, or family members? Discuss with him the importance of using his eyes, pointing out that doing so makes other people feel good, and that what he says matters. You can make a game out of this task for young children by role playing with stuffed animals or puppets. Discussing how nodding his head or use of fillers such as "Uh huh" can help the speaker feel as though the child is truly listening and understands his message. Take turns with the puppets, doing it with animation!

Rule 2: Speaking with Eye Contact

Children need to use eye contact when speaking to others.

Reason

Decreased eye contact negatively effects communication. It is important for children to use their eyes, as well as their bodies, when speaking to others. The feedback they get from the listener also helps in the development of perspective-taking. The eyes give us very valuable information about how other people are feeling and what they might be thinking, when combined with body language and facial expressions.

The reasoning for difficulties with determining facial expressions can be widely speculated about. Young children who have social difficulties may simply be more absorbed in themselves and their own wants and needs to use their eyes, or they may find making eye contact simply too visually overstimulating. Older children may be deterred from watching people's faces because their self-esteem has been damaged over time by observing faces that reflect confusion, frustration, or disappointment. Whatever the catalyst, as these children grow older, they often have a hard time understanding facial expressions and body language.

Direct social coaching involves explaining these facial expressions, gestures, and body postures succinctly and clearly.

Vocabulary

- After teaching the importance of this rule, cue with "Are you talking to me? You were not looking at me, so I was not sure…"

- When child is speaking to a peer, cue with "What is your friend's face telling you?"

- Later on, decrease cue to "Use your eyes."

TIPS

Does the child make eye contact when speaking to you or does he avoid your gaze? Is he able to identify the emotions he may evoke in others, either positive or negative? Does he repair misunderstandings that may occur or when his speech and language is unclear to others? Try playing emotion charades with younger children so that they become more comfortable seeing different facial expressions in a playful manner.

Rule 3: Using Eyes to Ask Yes/No Questions

After asking a yes/no question, the child must wait and listen with eyes and ears to avoid missing the answer he is seeking.

Reason

Children with social skill delays have been observed to perhaps ask a "Yes" or "No" question of others; however, they do not use their eyes to "hear the answer." As a result, they will often ask the same question multiple times while continuing with what they are doing and ignoring listener with their eyes. Scaffolding the skills for using their eyes effectively is something that can easily be taught and then paired with positive reinforcement with the child sees a smiling/loving face.

Vocabulary

- After discussing this rule, cue with "Ask a question and then look for the answer."

- And then later, "Look for the answer."

- Then, "Wait for the answer!"

TIPS

Observe the child's stimulability for this particular rule. Is he able to ask once and wait for the answer with his eyes? If not, for a set period of time, do the following: When the child asks a "Yes" or "No" question, respond nonverbally by either nodding or shaking your head. (Begin by using this task when the answer to his particular question is "Yes." When done with a warm and loving facial expression, you will increase the self-reinforcing tendency of the child to use his eyes when speaking with you.) Then cue the child with one of the above vocabulary tips, such as "Look for the answer!" This is a self-reinforcing task, especially if the answer is the one the child is hoping for!

Rule 4: Entering Play Already Underway

When entering a group situation, a child must use his eyes and ears to "get up to speed" with the play at hand.

Reason

Even when a child is able to initiate social interaction, such as joining a group of peers, his social work is not yet done. He needs to use his visual modality when he enters a play situation to greet his friends and then find his role in the play at hand. In social coaching sessions, we have observed children who come in and interrupt the play by talking about themselves or a game they want to play. Others have a tough time "getting up to speed" regarding what exactly is going on. If the child was not present for the start of an activity, he will remain on the periphery of play. This is a skill that, when focused on in session, can be worked on to achieve successful social play.

Vocabulary

- Taking the time to assess the situation by using his eyes, ears, and brain will give the child the information necessary to make an informed decision as to whether to join in play or leave.

- Begin by having the child join in with "What are you playing?" then simply watch for a while.

- Later they may want to ask, "Can I play next?"

- Social coaching includes helping the children make good judgments regarding what situation they should get themselves into. For example, if after watching a game it feels as though the kids are playing too roughly or the players are getting tense, it would *not* be a good idea for the child to enter.

TIPS

When a child enters a room you are in and begins asking you a question *despite* what you are doing, prompt him by saying, "Wait. Use your eyes and ears first and then ask me a question." Afterwards, have him tell you what was going on in the room when he entered (who was there, what he/she was doing, etc.) and have him explain whether that was a good time to ask his question.

Rule 5: Localizing Sound with Eyes

It is important for children to use their eyes and ears when in a group setting in order to know who is talking.

Reason

If another child makes a comment or statement, only by using his eyes and ears together can a child localize the sound source and recognize to whom the other child is speaking.

- *Scenario One:* A child who is anxious knows he is in a group and will fall back on the idea that "someone else" will answer. We have had to impress upon children that they are not going unnoticed. To the group they are just "the unusually quiet kids."

- *Scenario Two:* There are also children who answer every question presented. As social coaches we believe that a child who uses his eyes with his ears will definitely manage to find his "place" in a group—to find himself in space and in relation to peers in the room.

Vocabulary

- After teaching the importance of this lesson, cue with "[Child's Name], listen with your eyes."

- Decrease cue to "Listen with your eyes."

- Also, "Your friend will be looking at who they are asking. Let's watch!"

- If he missed the question, cue him to "Ask if they can repeat what they said."

TIPS

Observe the child you are working with over the next week. Does he use his eyes and ears together when in a group? If not, which of the above scenarios best describes the social breakdown? Use the above vocabulary tips to help foster use of both visual and auditory modalities (sense of sight and sense of hearing) when in a group situation.

Rule 6: Shifting Gaze when in Group

It is important for children to shift their gaze when speaking to more than one person.

Reason

When conversing with more than one person it is important that children realize they need to shift their gaze back and forth between those in the group. Doing so shows respect for the group and lets the speaker know that you are listening. For our children with social skill deficits, it allows them to observe the facial expressions, gestures, and body positioning of those in the group. This skill provides the child with vital information for participating in a conversation successfully.

Vocabulary

- After discussing this rule, cue with gesture of finger in a circle at eye level and to "Tell both/all of us your story. It makes us feel good when you look at all of us."

- Then give the gestural cue paired with verbal cue of "Tell both/all of us."

- Finally, decrease the cue to only gestural cue.

TIPS

Observe the child while you are speaking with two or more people. Is the child able to appropriately shift his gaze back and forth between between the speaker and listener(s)? Young children will often find an adult and address him or her, while excluding peers. Social coaches will then cue using the above vocabulary, and then slide behind a peer in order to help shift the child's gaze to his friend. When the peer listens with interest, this positively reinforces the child and the goal tends to generalize more quickly.

Rule 7: Using Gaze to Track

It is important for children to use visual tracking to follow the gaze of another.

Reason

Tracking the gaze of others is an important social skill as it helps fill in information when verbal cues are not present. For example, when someone is addressing a person but not using his name to get his attention, another child present may incorrectly think that he is the one being spoken to. Tracking the speaker's eye gaze will tell us whom is being addressed.

Also, sometimes when adults talk they will reference something, not by labeling it verbally, but by glancing over at it, and then continue talking. If our children are not aware that one's eyes also function as "arrows," they are bound to miss important information in the classroom and other settings.

Vocabulary

- After discussing this rule, cue with "Watch my eyes. I am looking at [name] and talking to them."

- Then decrease cue to "Who am I looking at?"

- Or "Follow my eyes."

TIPS

Make a game out of teaching this particular rule. Take turns with one of you gazing at an object somewhere in the room and the others guessing what it is the person is looking at. Start with large objects and then decrease the size of the objects in order to increase the level of difficulty. This particular rule is also important in the development of perspective-taking. Adjust the name of this game to "What am I Thinking About Now?" with older children. This links the concept of what the person is thinking about with what he is currently looking at. Again, bump up the level of difficulty by asking, "Why am I thinking about this object?" Example: Clock. "Because you are wondering what time it is?"

Chapter Six

Emotional Regulation

Rule 1: Understanding Likes/Dislikes

Children need to be able to express their own likes and dislikes.

Reason

Children with developmental delays may not cognitively have considered what they like and dislike. In order to know how they feel about certain things emotionally, they need to know what they hold important or discard as unimportant to them. This can be taught either individually with a child or in a peer group. A group setting sometimes allows for more conversation by sparking in another ideas of what she likes/dislikes.

Vocabulary

- After reviewing this concept, cue with "Is that something that you like/dislike? Your face tells me you are very [emotion] about it."

- Then, "Your face tells me that this is something you care about/dislike greatly."

- Finally, "How do you feel about [the object/situation]?"

- Decrease further to thumbs up/thumbs down gesture.

TIPS

You could work on making a list of things an individual child likes or dislikes.

With younger children use of thumbs up/thumbs down gesture can be helpful. Provide suggestions such as colors, food, sports, cartoon characters, or shows.

With older children, making a collage together can be a helpful activity. The adult could also make one of her own to show that people often have different likes/dislikes. Once the idea has been taught, work on this concept in a peer group setting. This again allows for the child to see that many people have different likes/dislikes, but children of the same age may also have a number of things in common.

Rule 2: Tone of Voice

Children must learn to use appropriate tone of voice with peers.

Reason

While this particular rule can also fall under perspective-taking, use of tone of voice with peers is often a difficulty with emotional regulation. When a child is caught up in the emotional turmoil in her brain and body she is not truly present and, thus, perspective-taking goes by the wayside. Social coaching systematically teaches how our tone of voice changes depending on to whom and where we are talking (for example: teacher v. baby and library v. baseball game).

Vocabulary

- When a child speaks, she often does not realize how it sounds and may be perceived by others. For example, a child may say "Give!" when wanting something. This is a learning opportunity and should not be overlooked.

- Rather, act confused, and calmly state, "Give? What does that mean? I don't understand." This may frustrate and emotionally disregulate a child, resulting in crying or screaming. Prompt her by saying, "Please give me..." and wait for her to complete the sentence.

- Once the child understands your expectation for a full sentence when making a request or statement in the right tone, it is important to be less directive in the prompts. If the statement is still not acceptable, simply re-state, "Try again" until it is done appropriately, then positively reinforce thereafter. This prompt requires the child to figure out on her own what the problem is and how to correct it.

TIPS

This particular vocabulary cue has been helpful for a great many children. As adults, we know that when a child is aware of what needs to occur verbally and socially, the use of the phrase "Try again" allows her to think, process, and successfully correct it herself. It is critical the situation be followed up with positive reinforcement. This can be as obvious as verbal praise or as subtle as a smile, nod, thumbs up, or high five.

Rule 3: Understanding One's Own Emotions

Children need to be able to identify emotions within themselves.

Reason

Many of the children seen for social coaching are unable to label how it is they are feeling. They often understand only a handful of emotions, such as happy/sad/mad, and are lacking more in-depth knowledge of what they feel. By systematically learning about a wide variety of emotions and talking about them and situations in which she has felt that way, the child gains power over herself and her environment. Also, the ability to verbally label their own emotions often helps children by diffusing the nature of strong emotions, such as anger and frustration.

Vocabulary

- After teaching this rule, cue with "Your face is telling me that you are [emotion]. Do you feel [emotion]?"

- "Your body is showing me that you are [emotion]."

TIPS

To teach this particular rule, begin by pairing the way in which the child is presenting with the emotion she may be feeling. An example of this task could be picking a crayon color out of the box and then drawing a face which represents the color. (Red for angry, Blue for sad, Yellow for happy, etc.) Then discuss with the child an instance in which she felt that particular emotion and how she expressed it. Was she able to tell anyone how she felt? If not, was she then frustrated? There are also a number of great books for children sold in stores that discuss a wide variety of emotions (e.g. Cain 2005; Offerman and Moroney 1999; Parr 2000; Wilson-Max 1999). Read these books aloud in front of a mirror and practice making the faces being discussed.

Rule 4: Understanding Emotions of Others

Children need to be able to identify the emotions of others and label them.

Reason

In order for a child to be socially successful, it is important that she be able to identify the emotions of others. This is the beginning of developing empathy for peers. It is also the ability through which we are able to gauge how to address other people/how we reply to others. Be sure Rules 1–3 in this chapter have been discussed before embarking on this particular area of emotional regulation.

Vocabulary

- After discussing the importance of this particular rule, begin by asking, "How do you think your friend is feeling? What can we say to him?"

- Discuss also, "Why do you think your friend is feeling [emotion]?"

- Decrease cue finally to "Check in with your friend."

TIPS

For younger children, role playing is a helpful activity as it displaces heavy emotions from their own personal situation. They are often able to express emotions they themselves are not comfortable with by using puppets/stuffed animals. With older children, games such as emotional charades can be helpful and fun at the same time. Also, when reading aloud to children, discuss how the characters may be feeling and why. Have the children imitate the emotions that the character is feeling, and perhaps share a time when they felt that way.

Rule 5: Appearance of Emotions on Self

Children need to realize how their feelings are being represented in their own facial expressions and body postures.

Reason

Many of the children who receive social coaching are completely unaware of how their own face and body present to others. Regardless of whether a child is in "freeze," "flight," or "fight," her thoughts are engaged in herself and how her body feels. This particular rule must be taught when the child is calm and involved in a favorite or preferred task. This will help the child to cognitively process the information with the hope that when in the lower cortex of her brain, where freeze/flight/fight occurs, her thoughts might be brought back up to the upper cortex, and she will be able to remember that she does have control over emotional social situations.

Vocabulary

- When the child is calm, go back and revisit a situation in which there was high emotion for the child. Discuss alternative ways in which the child could have responded.

- When in the middle of an emotionally charged situation, attempt to distract or redirect the child in order to engage the cognitive part of the brain, rather than the flight/fight/freeze portion.

TIPS

Task one

Read a book about a child who is expressing high emotion, such as *What Are You So Grumpy About* by Tom Lichtenheld (2007). Discuss with the child what it means to have "balled fists," a "pinched face," "hands on hips," "head in their hands." Drawing out the characters on paper and writing the emotions underneath is also a helpful task.

Task two

When talking about emotions does your child usually rely on telling you what she *thinks* versus how she is *feeling*? See the above vocabulary tips to help her distinguish between the two. Often a variety of emotions must first be taught, as children might truly not be certain what it is they are feeling inside.

Rule 6: Emotional Situations

Children must learn to first experience a situation, then cognitively process the situation, and then respond accordingly.

Reason

This is not intended to minimize the child's true emotions but to help her learn. We do not want her going from A to C, but rather going through the process of cognition, allowing her access to A to B to C. In doing so, social coaching gives her the boost in confidence to know she does have control over herself and her environment.

Vocabulary

- After a situation of high emotion occurs wait until later to discuss it with the child. When the child is calm, discuss with her the idea that "The situation felt like a big deal right when it happened, but that feeling went away, and then it felt more like a 'little deal.' Can you wait and see if that is the same next time?"

- Next time, cue with "It feels like a 'big deal' but that feeling will pass soon."

- "Is it a 'big deal' or 'little deal'?"

- Finally, decrease cue to use of a gesture of fingers spread apart a small distance to symbolize a "small deal."

TIPS

Often the children we see with social developmental delays also demonstrate emotional delays. As a result, when something occurs that they are not expecting and/or do not like, their response is not proportionate to the event itself. We stress that while things may really seem big at the time, they lessen over a given period of time. While it is hard to talk about emotional situations initially at that juncture, we suggest parents/professionals wait until later, when the emotional level is not as high and when they can look back clearly and reflect.

As they improve with this particular rule of emotional regulation, we use a finger and thumb gesture to help defuse an immediate difficulty. The thumb and pointer finger are spaced an inch or so apart to represent a "small deal." Your social coach can let you know how this prompt is being received in sessions so that you can be reassured when the child is more ready for just a visual prompt of "big deal" versus "little deal."

Rule 7: Embarrassment

Children need to know how to recognize the feeling of embarrassment and learn to work through it.

Reason

All humans have the propensity to become embarrassed when they feel they have said or done the wrong thing in a social setting. The important thing for children to realize is that the embarrassment will decrease given time. For children with social skill delays the feeling of embarrassment can be overwhelming. For some children, embarrassment can put them in to a state of flight/fright/freeze. Social coaching helps children understand the feeling and to know that with time it will go away. Again, the use of "big deal" v. "small deal" can be helpful. (See previous rule.)

Vocabulary

- Ask the child if the situation was a "big deal" or a "small deal." If she answers "big deal," rephrase with something such as "If your friend did [situation], would you think he is stupid? No? Okay, so let me ask you again, is this a 'big deal' or a 'little deal'?"

- Next time, cue with "It feels like a 'big deal' but that feeling will pass soon."

- "Is it a 'big deal' or 'little deal'?"

- Finally, decrease the cue to the use of a gesture of fingers spread apart a small distance to symbolize a "small deal."

TIPS

Often adults do not say outright, "I am so embarrassed." Using internal dialogue out loud can help children who have not picked up the skills to deal with this tough emotion on their own. Embarrassment is hard enough as an adult but as an elementary school child it can seem devastating. In the upcoming weeks, verbally dialogue how you yourself are feeling (with some exaggeration of body posture and facial expressions) when feeling embarrassed, but verbalize how the feeling goes away when you realized it was not really a "big deal," just an event that happened and will soon be forgotten.

Rule 8: Human Relatedness

Children need to learn verbal turn-taking with the overall goal of human relatedness.

Reason

Once a child becomes more comfortable in a peer group setting, she is then able to increase her pursuit of human relatedness. The desire to interact and maintain a mutually reciprocal conversation demands that our children reach a higher level in understanding the perspectives of others. It is crucial, however, that the desire for relating with another peer be there in order for our children with social skill delays to begin receiving coaching of higher-level verbal turn-taking.

Vocabulary

Social coaching through this model advocates supporting from the sidelines once the children have obtained this level of human relatedness to help foster perspective-taking. When a breakdown in verbal turn-taking occurs, such as a message being misunderstood by another peer, cue with "Pause" or "Freeze" in an attempt to rewind and go back and try the interaction again in a safe and supportive environment.

TIPS

Observe the child when you converse with her. Are your conversations one-sided, with the child going on about a favorite topic without really expecting you to verbally respond? We have all spoken with another person who seemed to actually be waiting for you as speaker to stop talking so that she could say what she wanted. We encourage parents and professionals to find mutually enjoyable topics such as an outing or event that would entice the child to have a reciprocal conversation more spontaneously.

Chapter Seven

Developing Humor

Rule 1: Understanding Rules of Laughter

If a child is laughing while in a group, he must be sure others understand why he is laughing.

Reason

Often children on the autism spectrum are preoccupied with things on their mind, and are not always present or relational; it is a great deal of work for them to be so. As a result, they may laugh out loud when nothing funny has been said. Other children become aware of this behavior around four or five years of age and may veer away from those who laugh at inappropriate times. It is important to explain directly to the child that when he is in a group he can laugh, but he needs to explain to his peers why he is doing so in order to avoid hurting anyone's feelings.

Vocabulary

- After discussing this rule, cue with "Share with the group what is funny."

- Decrease cue when possible to "You are laughing…" This is intended to get the child to monitor himself and make a social repair straight away.

- If another child believes he is being laughed at, cue the person who was laughing to "Look at your friend's face. What can you say to him?"

TIPS

Take the opportunity to observe the child at play with peers. Is he involved in parallel play with peers? Does he laugh out loud while playing with others for unexplained reasons? Does he appear nervous or anxious when doing so, or is he unaware of the laughter's effect on others? Take the time to explain that this is not okay to do ("Just so you know…"), as others might feel as though he is laughing at them. Then cue as outlined above in vocabulary tips.

Rule 2: Power of Humor

A child must learn that he has the power to make other people laugh and feel good.

Reason

Some of the children we see are serious by nature. For children with social skill delays, levity is not often something that comes naturally to them. We encourage these children to laugh and be silly and to know that they have the power to make others laugh. This plays a critical role in supporting the development of human relatedness as the children begin truly to enjoy the company of others. At this point in peer groups, the children will become more interested in each other and not as much in the specific task in which they are involved.

Vocabulary

- After discussing this rule with the child, cue with "Look at your friend's face. You made her laugh!" This helps pair his words with the expression he has helped place on another's face.

- To reinforce attempts at humor you can help by identifying them as humorous. For example, "You have a good sense of humor. You made us all laugh."

TIPS

Encourage your child to laugh and be humorous during playful interactions. Tell him when something he did is funny to you. The next step is to push beyond that particular level of play so the child continues to develop his sense of humor and his development of play simultaneously.

Rule 3: Literal v. Non-Literal Language

Children need to understand the difference between literal language and non-literal language.

Reason

Children need to understand that not everything they hear or read is meant literally. Children with social development delays typically do not pick up information from their environment easily, rather they need to be taught the information and to practice one to one before generalization can begin. The idea of language being anything other than literal is confusing for children with pragmatic language delays.

Beginning as early as three or four years of age discussing literal versus non-literal language will help these children to grasp that not everything means exactly what it seems. Much of our use of language is not literal, such as "Her smile is like sunshine," "Go out on a limb," "Pull an idea out of the air," or "Get a jump on it."

Vocabulary

- Teach the idea of non-literal language by giving examples appropriate to the child's developmental age. Then cue with "Is that what it really means? Or does it mean something else?"

- Once the idea is emerging as a receptive skill, cue with "Did I really mean____?"

TIPS

Observe how concrete the child is with his use and understanding of language. Begin to introduce phrases the child may identify with and hear in day-to-day life, such as "Take a seat." The use of pictures can also be helpful as he puts a visual to the silliness of the idioms himself.

Rule 4: Experimenting with Humor

With guidance, children should experiment with humor.

Reason

Children need to understand humor and the ability to use it appropriately at the right time and place. Typically, children around five years of age begin making nonsensical jokes. As they are developing these skills, the jokes will at times be awkward and difficult for the listener to understand. When children have significant delays in social development, they may begin to experiment with humor at an older age. Many times this spike in humor development occurs in elementary school. As we typically expect the level of humor in this age group to be quite complex, a child who is just working on this skill may seem immature and unsure. He may make remarks that are offensive or confusing. It is important for parents and social coaches to guide children through this process in order to help avoid misunderstandings with peers and ruining current or potential friendships.

Vocabulary

- After discussing the importance of this rule, cue with "Check your friend's face" to be sure the joke was not misunderstood.

- Also, "Did your friend think that was funny? Or is he [emotion]?"

- Later cue with "Check in with your friend."

TIPS

Knock knock jokes are a good starting place for introducing humor to children. Also, simple riddles or puns for kids can be a fun way of teaching humor. Your local library should have a number of joke books for children. These will help the child get a jump start on literal language versus non-literal language. (It also can help scaffold the children's thinking toward understanding inference as they grow older.)

Rule 5: Effect of Humor on Others

Children around age six must watch the faces of others to see if their humor has taken correctly.

Reason

As children enter elementary school, they are around peers in the classroom, at lunch, and at recess. Vernacular language begins to circulate around them and most children on the autism spectrum and/or with Sensory Processing Disorder do not understand the fast-paced nature of this dialogue. While they are developing their sense of humor at age five and six, their jokes may not always come off as funny. They need to use their visual modality to judge the facial expression or body posture of friends around them to see how their jokes were received and to be able to repair and move on from there.

Vocabulary

- After discussing the importance of this rule, cue with "Check your friend's face. What is it telling you?"

- Decrease the cue to "Check with your friend."

- If the child is at all uncertain about how his joke might be received he is instructed to insert "Just kidding" after his attempt at humor.

TIPS

Observe your child or client with friends to see if he is utilizing non-literal language and humor with peers. If so, how is his humor received by others? Is he able to repair if a joke falls flat? The need to foster this skill is important in order to preserve friendships made and potential future relationships.

Social Skills Checklist

Child:	D.O.B.:
Date:	Person completing form:

Based on parent/professional observation, rate the child's skill level in the seven program criteria. See the rating scale below. Put a check mark in the box that best represents the child's current level. The "Priority" Box should be checked for rules that the adult determines are important future goals for the child.

- **Almost always** = The child consistently demonstrates this skill in various settings and with a variety of people.

- **Often** = The child displays this skill in a few settings and with a few people.

- **Sometimes** = The child may demonstrate this skill occasionally.

- **Almost never** = The child never/rarely displays this skill.

Chapter One: Initiating Social Interaction	Almost always	Often	Sometimes	Almost never	Priority
1. Greets others					
2. Initiates joint attention					
3. Asks for help					
4. Responds to comments					
5. Shares ideas and accomplishments					
6. Asks questions					
7. Gets clarification					
8. Asks someone to play					
9. Initiates conversation					
10. Repairs misunderstandings					

Chapter Two: Maintaining Social Interaction	Almost always	Often	Sometimes	Almost never	Goal
1. Able to make small transitions					
2. Able to make large transitions					
3. Maintains play					
4. Uses turn-taking					
5. Watches peers take their turn					
6. Demonstrates organized play					
7. Decides who goes first					
8. Negotiates with peers					
9. Navigates misunderstandings					
10. Appropriately quits a game/exits a group					

Chapter Three: Body Positioning	Almost always	Often	Sometimes	Almost never	Priority
1. Keeps body in the group					
2. Exits the group appropriately					
3. Uses appropriate body positioning					
4. Uses words, not hands/body to communicate					
5. Asks and waits for the answer					
6. Understands idea of personal space					

Chapter Four: Perspective-Taking	Almost always	Often	Sometimes	Almost never	Priority
1. Thinks about others' likes/ dislikes					
2. Uses pronouns "you"/"we"/"us"					
3. Positions objects in relation to self and others					
4. Understands own effect on the emotions of others					
5. Acknowledges comments of others					
6. Reads body cues of others					
7. Uses clarification when laughter occurs					
8. Expresses empathy					

Chapter Five: Visual Modality	Almost always	Often	Sometimes	Almost never	Priority
1. Uses appropriate eye contact when listening					
2. Uses appropriate eye contact when speaking					
3. Uses eyes when asking yes/no questions					
4. Enters play already underway					
5. Localizes to sound with both eyes and ears					
6. Shifts gaze when in a group					
7. Uses gaze to track					

Chapter Six: Emotional Regulation	Almost always	Often	Sometimes	Almost never	Priority
1. Understands the likes/dislikes of others					
2. Uses appropriate tone of voice					
3. Understands their own feelings					
4. Identifies emotions of others					
5. Understands that their emotions are represented in own facial expressions/body postures					
6. Responds appropriately in emotional situations					
7. Deals with embarrassment appropriately					
8. Demonstrates human relatedness					

Chapter Seven: Development of Humor	Almost always	Often	Sometimes	Almost never	Priority
1. Understands laughter					
2. Sees power in making others laugh					
3. Understands literal v. non-literal language					
4. Experiments with humor					
5. Watches expressions of others to see if they are laughing					

Bibliography

American Psychiatric Association (2000) *Diagnostic and Statistical Manual of Mental Disorders* (4th edition). Washington, DC: APA.

Ayers, A.J. (2005) *Sensory Integration and the Child* (25th anniversary edition). Los Angeles, CA: Western Psychological Services.

Baron-Cohen, S., Tager-Flusberg, H. and Cohen, D. (2000). *Understanding Other Minds: Perspectives from Developmental Cognitive Neuroscience.* New York, NY: Oxford University Press, Inc.

Cain, J. (2005) *The Way I Feel.* Seattle, WA: Parenting Press, Inc.

Garcia Winner, M. (2007) *Thinking About You Thinking About Me* (2nd edition). San Jose, CA: Think Social Publishing, Inc.

Greenspan, S. and Wieder, S. (2006) *Engaging Autism.* Cambridge, MA: Da Capo Press.

Kowalski, T.P. (2002) *The Source for Asperger's Syndrome.* East Moline, IL: LinguiSystems, Inc.

Levine, M. (2002) *A Mind at a Time.* New York, NY: Simon and Schuster.

Lichtenheld, T. (2007) *What Are You So Grumpy About.* New York, NY: Little, Brown Books for Young Readers.

Miller, L.J. (2006) *Sensational Kids*. New York, NY: Penguin Group.

Offerman, L. and Moroney, T. (1999) *Little Teddy Bear's Happy Face Sad Face: A First Book About Feelings*. Brookfield, CT: Millbrook Press, Inc.

Ostovar, R. (2009) *The Ultimate Guide to Sensory Processing Disorder: Easy, Everyday Solutions to Sensory Challenges*. Arlington, TX: Sensory World.

Parr, T. (2000) *The Feelings Book*. New York, NY: Little, Brown and Company.

Paul, R. (1995) *Language Disorders from Infancy through Adolescence: Assessment and Intervention*. St. Louis, MO: Mosby.

Rapee, R., Wignall, A., Spence, S., Cobham, V. and Lyneham, H. (2008) *Helping Your Anxious Child* (2nd edition). Oakland, CA: New Harbinger Publications, Inc.

Richard, G.J. (2001) *The Source for Processing Disorders*. East Moline, IL: LinguiSystems, Inc.

Wilson-Max, K. (1999) *L is for Loving*. New York, NY: Hyperion Books for Children.

Index

likes
    thinking about
        others' 69–70
    understanding
        101–2
listening, with eye
    contact 87–8,
    91, 95

misunderstandings
    clarifying 28–9,
        82–3
    over humor 123
    during play 53–4
    repairing 34–5, 90
Moroney, T. 106
motor imitation 20

negotiating, during play
    47, 51–2

objects
    carrier 39
    commenting on 78
    gazing game 100
    positioning 74–5
Offerman, L. 106

palms up 51–2, 65
parallel play 30, 39
Parr, T. 106
passing mentions,
    responding to 22
pause, as a cue 115
peers
    getting attention of
        24–5
    sharing with 32
    watching at play
        45–6
    personal space 67–8
    see also body
        positioning

perspective-taking
    69–85
    acknowledging
        comments 78–9
    affecting emotions
        of others 76–7
    clarifying "why are
        you laughing?"
        82–3
    expressing empathy
        84–5
    positioning of
        objects and items
        74–5
    reading body cues
        80–1
    thinking about
        others 69–71
    tone of voice 103–4
    use of pronouns
        72–3
    when watching
        peers at play 45
Pervasive
    Developmental
    Disorder-Not
    Otherwise
    Specified (PDD-
    NOS) 11
plans
    back-up 83
    flexible 40, 47
play
    asking someone to
        30–1
    entering play
        already
        underway 93–4
    group 57–8
    maintaining 37–56
        exiting 55–6
        maintaining play
        41–2
        navigating mis-
        understand-
        ings 53–4

negotiating 47,
    51–2
organizing 47–8
transitions, large
    39–40
transitions, small
    37–8
turn-taking 43–4
watching peers at
    45–6
who goes first
    49–50
parallel 30
sharing during 24–5
play acting
    and body
    positioning 62
    with figures 58, 60
    and showing
    empathy 85
positioning
    of objects and items
        74–5
    see also body
    positioning
positive reinforcement
    25, 33, 79, 91,
    98, 104
pragmatic difficulties 57
Pragmatic Language
    Disorder 13
preschool 32, 63, 68
pronouns, use of 72–3
puns 124
puppets, in role play 88,
    108

questions, asking 26–7,
    51
    "ask a question" cue
        21, 67, 72
    for clarification
        28–9
    and waiting for the
        answer 65–6
    yes/no 91–2